PRAY, PRAISE AND HOORAY

Concordia Publishing House, St. Louis, Missouri
Concordia Publishing House Ltd., London, E. C. 1
Copyright © 1972 Concordia Publishing House
Library of Congress Catalog Card No. 77-175306
ISBN 0-570-03130-3

MANUFACTURED IN THE UNITED STATES OF AMERICA

PRAY, PRAISE AND HOORAY

BY RICHARD BIMLER

CONCORDIA PUBLISHING HOUSE-ST. LOUIS-LONDON

PRAYERS FOR YOUTH AND OTHER PEOPLE

These prayers might best be described as a little creative fooling around with how we communicate with our Lord. They are not intended to cover all of the areas of youth's concerns and joys, but we do hope they hit some of the high spots of life. The underlying theme of the booklet is the hooray-ness of our relationship with our living Lord. To love our Lord and be loved by Him is to affirm life and get excited about living each day to its fullest as we share this love and joy with other people God has put around us.

This is not to be merely a book of religious words and clichés but instead a source of fresh ideas and feelings to consider and relate to one's own life. The words, phrases, slogans, and pictures are visuals to aid you in seeing all of life as celebration and joy! Let's celebrate — great!

The blank pages are not to show that the author ran out of words. Rather it is hoped that the reader will want to scratch out some of his own prayer thoughts, feelings, joys, and concerns that might come to mind as he flips through these pages. And why not even look for other words, slogans, and pictures that might apply to your own feelings and prayers related to you in these thoughts?

This book is organized under various "Big Words" which youth themselves selected as areas of concern, need, and joy in terms of their prayer life. I thank the youth of the parish for writing the table of contents for me!

This booklet also supposes that prayer is not only an act of a person of God but also a relationship we have with our Lord, that prayers are said and whispered and shouted and lived out as we go about our daily lives. A Christian lives in prayer, and therefore prayer is *being* something rather than merely *doing* something. And now before some of you start murmuring your own thoughts such as: "When will this introduction ever cease?" we shall conclude these remarks and get on with our little tidbits of prayers. And you don't even need to fold your hands as you read this through—it's especially hard to turn the pages in that situation!

Let us *Pray, Praise, and HOORAY* each day of our lives!

RICH BIMLER

These HOORAY prayers are dedicated to some of the HOORAY people in my life—Hazel, Diane, Bobby, and Mike

50 BIG WORDS OF TODAY

AND MORE AS YOU GO ALONG!

1. Acceptance   16
2. Advertisements   17
3. Baptism   18
4. Bible   20
5. Bumper Stickers   24
6. Celebration and Joy   25
7. Change   28
8. Christmas   30
9. Church   35
10. Communion   37
11. Confirmation   38
12. Death   39
13. Doubt   41
14. Easter   43
15. Ecology   45
16. Failure   46
17. Family   47
18. Forgiveness   49
19. Graduation   50
20. Hunger   51
21. Hypocrisy   53
22. Identity   54
23. Incidentals   56
24. Laughter   58
25. Life   59
26. Loneliness   65
27. Love   66
28. Money   67
29. Morning   68
30. Movies   70
31. New Year   73
32. Occupation   74
33. People   75
34. Pictures   79
35. Politics   81
36. Popcorn   82
37. Prayer   83
38. Priorities   89

39. Problems   90
40. Respect   92
41. Response-ability   93
42. School   94
43. Songs   99
44. Sports   101
45. Summer   102
46. War and Peace   104
47. Words   105
48. World   106
49. Worship   108
50. Youth   113

A PRAYER BOOK NEVER ENDS

Prayer

IS...

A PRAYER IS . . . a relationship with God.

A PRAYER IS . . . a way of knowing that God is with you.

A PRAYER IS . . . a bunch of words, often meaningless, offered up to God in hopes that they find meaning.

A PRAYER IS . . . anything you want to share with your Lord.

A PRAYER IS . . . a desire shared with our God-sized man in hopes of ridding ourself of our man-sized gods.

A PRAYER IS . . . a way God comes down to us and brings us back up to Him.

A PRAYER IS . . . Direct Distance Dialing to our Father.

A PRAYER IS . . . a chance to know that Someone really cares, in spite of.

A PRAYER IS . . . like love: it must be expressed in action and not only in words.

A PRAYER IS . . . a God's-eye view of man.

A PRAYER IS . . . a way, not to get something, but a way to be with Someone.

A PRAYER IS . . . knowing that you'll never be alone in this world.

A PRAYER IS . . . relating God to a situation and then seeing His power and love.

A PRAYER IS . . . a way, not to change God but to let God change us.

A PRAYER IS . . . !

I. ACCEPTANCE

ACCEPT OR EXCEPT, LORD?

Lord, I like to think that I accept everyone for what they are. But if I really get honest, I'd have to say that I accept everyone with exceptions.

What I mean to say is that it's easy to love and accept everyone in general. But it's a little harder for me to accept an individual who's standing next to me whom I can't seem to really like because of some peculiarity or habit.

But it's not a laughing matter, is it, Lord? I need help in accepting the unacceptable (by my standards, anyway). I need help in seeing all people the way You see all people.

Lord, give me Your eyes when I look at people. Give me Your love when I must deal with all types of people. Give me Your patience to understand and accept the people around me, like parents and friends and teachers, neighbors, salesmen, bus drivers, and little brothers.

I know You accept me as I am, Lord. Thanks.

Now let me see people Cross-eyed—as I look at them through Your death and resurrection for me. Then, and only then, can I really accept the people You have put into my daily life!

2. ADVERTISEMENTS

ADVERTISEMENTS

Lord, why are ads more alive than churches these days?

Ads bombard us from all sides. Some statistics say that over 1,400 a day hit us seeking our loyalties.

Not all ads are bad, Lord. Of course, not all ads are good either. Some try to make how I smell more important than my relationship to You.

Some seem to say that salvation in life comes through a soft drink, a new pair of underwear, or some facial cream.

But other ads, Lord, really help me to see You more alive in life. They give joy and love for people and new excitement in being what You have made me.

Lord, help me to use ads as visual reminders that You are really present in this world. Help me to see You alive in people and events happening each day.

Speak to me, Lord, through the avenue of ads each day.

Help all people to catch the excitement and joy of knowing You. And You're free too, Lord; no coupons to send in, no need for trial offers.

I'm sold on You!

CALL ROTO ROOTER

3. BAPTISM

BAPTISM

No man is an island, Lord; we're all brought together by water—the water of our baptism.

Thanks, Lord, for calling us Your people and by showing that You love us through our baptism.

Help me to rejoice each time I see a baptism happening in church. Help me to realize that I am also a part of each baptism—You are giving me more brothers and sisters.

Lord, it is kind of fun to watch a baptism happening. The parents are so concerned that little Charlie is going to scream. I like it when they scream, Lord. I would too if I were getting the devil knocked out of me!

The sponsors are worried that they say the right words and that they're loud enough. The head usher is trying desperately to remember if he remembered to put water in the font. And the pastor is struggling to recall what the baby's middle name is!

Baptism is a great happening in everyone's life, Lord. Help me to remember who I am each day by remembering my baptism each day. And help me to share the joys of this new birth with other people.

In baptism things happen. Thanks, Lord, for calling me by my first name!

THINGS I'D LIKE TO SHARE WITH GOD RIGHT NOW:

4. BIBLE

THE BIG FEED

Lord, I just heard the Gospel lesson read in church (John 6:1-15). And I need to rethink some thoughts. To think, here You fed all those people without asking any questions, like: Why didn't you eat before you came? or: Can't you buy your own lunch? And You didn't even take an offering to help defray the costs! You fed the people because they were hungry!

Lord, allow me to feed people (no matter what they hunger for) for no other reason except that they too are hungry!

THE GREAT GROCER IN THE SKY

Lord, You are more than a Bread King, more than the Great Grocer in the Sky. There is more to life than that!

How did You do the impossible task of feeding all those people?

Is it that You said 'thanks' and then used what God had given You? Is it that at first You accepted what You had and then shared it with others?

Help us to do the impossible too.

Help us to accept our fatness—and then help skinny people get fat.

Help us to do the impossible—by keeping our eyes on Your cross and empty tomb!

APOSTLES IN ACTION

Lord, thanks for naming the fifth book of the New Testament Acts. It sure makes sense.

We would be sunk if You had named it something like "The Resolutions of the Apostles" or "The Committee Meetings of the Apostles."

Help us to see that even the name of that book has a message in it for us.

And now help me as I continue in action for You!

SOMEBODY IS DOING SOMETHING

BOY — 1; DISCIPLES — 0

Lord, remember that little boy who gave You those little fish and loaves of bread that day when You had that picnic? I think I'd like to be like him. He reminds me of the time when I helped my dad buy my mom a birthday dress by giving him three of my hard-earned pennies. My wanting to help out far overshadowed the details of the cost of the dress.

I have nothing against Your disciples, Lord, except the Bible sure shows that they were kind of dumb at times. Like the time of the great picnic, when You fed the 5,000 out in the wilderness (I suppose there's a McDonald's there by now, though). Remember when Andrew and Philip laughed at that little boy who brought You that food? They were looking at the food shortage, and because of that You became unimportant to them at the time. But to the boy You were all-important, and therefore the vast food shortage became unimportant.

For once I'm glad I'm just a kid, Lord. Keep my priorities in balance. Keep my eyes on You rather than on just the problems of the day.

There sure is much food for thought here, Lord, isn't there?

There's a great chef near you

5. BUMPER STICKERS

BUMPER STICKER THEOLOGY

Lord, car bumpers have been one of the most creative and ingenious parts of Your whole creation. Look at all the theology that is read and absorbed on the highways each day through the medium of bumper stickers. Here are just a few I've seen recently:

> IS GOD IN YOUR DRIVER'S SEAT?
> ONE WAY WITH JESUS!
> IF YOU SPEED, WHY NOT SING "NEARER, MY GOD,
>   TO THEE"?
> CELEBRATE LIFE!
> SUPPORT YOUR LOCAL THEOLOGIAN
> CHRIST IS FOR PEOPLE, ARE YOU?
> IF YOU WON'T LET ME PRAY IN YOUR SCHOOL,
>   I WON'T LET YOU STUDY IN MY CHURCH!

Lord, thanks for bumper stickers. But don't let us rely on them too much to share our thoughts and feelings.

Make us all be communicators of Your Word and Your life with those we "bump" into in life. Help us to speak the Good Word to others in a very personal way too.

Hooray for bumper stickers, Lord, and hooray for the gifts of speaking and sharing Your love with others in every way possible!

Keep in our driver's seat, Lord!

6. CELEBRATION AND JOY

A QUICKIE

Lord, I just thought of something: Since You became human for me, I have become new man for You!

Hey, that's pretty great!

Thanks, Lord, I'll remember that today!

A HAPPY SERVICE

Lord, we had a youth service last Sunday in church.

And it really was a youth service. I mean, the kids just didn't usher or read the Scriptures and things, but we planned the entire service, we had a special youth presentation for the sermon, we passed out flowers and balloons as signs of joy and love, we sang our own kind of songs. But there have been some adults who didn't like it. And they are telling us about it, which is good, I guess. One reason for their criticism is that they didn't like the way we decorated the church—we had streamers and balloons and pictures all around the worship center to serve as a reminder that worship is joy and celebration in Christ's resurrection!

Lord, help me to understand those that accuse me. Help me to love and keep in touch with those who don't see worship and God the way I do. And, Lord, help all of us to see that there are balloons and streamers and pictures around each time we worship—it's just that sometimes we don't notice they are there!

FOR A HAPPIER LIFE

SMILE

A SMILE IS A SMILE IS A SMILE

Lord, what if I made a smile—and nobody came
         to see it?
Would it matter to anyone that I am happy?
Not Mrs. Jones,
who would rather go
to a garage sale
because you can buy
rugs
         and bugs
and pants
                  and ants
and suits
                  and fruits
and anything else valuable and necessary.
But how valuable is a smile, Lord?
What's in a smile?
Warmth,
         cheer,
love,
         happiness,
and anything else valuable and necessary.
But necessary for who?
(Or is that bad language?)

Lord, help us smile—that's the best language!
For me,
                  for him,
                           for her,
for us,
                  for them,
for all.   Amen.

7. CHANGE

CHANGE

Why do people fight change, Lord? Is it because they really don't understand the word?

Change is as necessary as breathing, isn't it, Lord? Yet nobody is interested in stopping his breathing. It seems that the word has a "bad" sound to it now, that change is evil.

But all of life is a change, Lord. I'm sure it is. Everything and everyone has to change to keep living. Look at the different seasons You give us; look at how relationships change; look at how people and places change. The only thing constant today is change itself!

Now I can already hear someone say that maybe things do change but that You, Lord, certainly do not. True, true, but my concept of You certainly changes. And this is good. I see You in a different way than I did when I was a 3-year-old and a 10-year-old and even when I was confirmed. My view of You changes as I gain more understanding of You and Your world.

Help people to see that even if they want things to stay the way they are, things are going to have to change!

Keep changing people, Lord. Remake us all so that we can accept Your constant love in this great world of change.

I'm not afraid of change, Lord, because You are You!

YOU'VE CHANGED. W

SPECIAL PRAYERS FOR SPECIAL PEOPLE

E'VE CHANGED

8. CHRISTMAS

CHRISTMAS IS . . . .

Lord, I heard a little boy remark in church that he didn't want to worship on Christmas morning because he hears his folks sing every Sunday, "Take me not away from my presents." Bless him, Lord, especially for his alertness and creativity.

THE "LIVE" MANGER SCENE

Some kids from the church's youth group portrayed another live manger scene this past week. Many people in cars came by to peek and see how cold the shepherds looked and how many were still holding out.

It's always amazed me, Lord, that in the live manger scenes of today the only person not "real" in these scenes is You. You are usually portrayed by a Raggedy Ann, a Baby First Step, or a Tippy Tumbles doll.

But that's really not true either, is it, Lord? Because You are alive in Cindy, who is playing Mary, and in Bob who is Joseph, and in Bruce, Doug, and Jane, who are decked out as the shepherds tonight. That's where You come alive—not in the crib but in people!

You make it truly a "live" manger scene! Help us to see You "alive" in all people every day!

NO GREATER LOVE

KEEP CHRIST IN X-MAS

Lord, it's Christmastime again, You know, the time for all "good" people to ridicule and criticize the commercialism of Christmas.

I'm tired of all the talk about commercialism, Lord. Why does everyone attack people who are trying to make a living? And why do people think that someone is going to take You away from Christmas? You're here to stay, Lord; Santa or no Santa, You're here. Help others to see that too.

Sure some people overdo it, Lord. Like the guy standing at his cash register singing, "What a Friend We Have in Jesus."

Help us all to see that You're always going to be in Christmas, whether we spell it X-mas or any other way.

Help me to look beyond the Santas and reindeers and snowmen and see You in the middle of my life whether I'm at Bethlehem, Calvary, or Chicago.

FREE CHRIST FROM CHRISTMAS!

Lord, when I see all of the Christmas decorations and customs around me, I can almost hear You shouting out: "Help! I'm being held captive in a manger!"

Why do You let us do that to You? Why do You let us keep you locked up in the manger scene as a little baby? Why do You let us put You away like churches put away their manger scenes for another year?

I know I shouldn't be blaming You, because we do it in spite of You, don't we? Maybe we like to treat You like ornaments and bells, because we can put You away whenever we want to.

And Christmas services sort of remind me of a sale at Sears or Macy's. You know, everyone flocks to the services to see the shepherds and Wise Men and to hear little Mike sing a cute little song. They don't want to miss anything. And then so many people don't come back until the next December "sale" hits again!

Help me to free You from Christmas, Lord. Help me to show others that You're alive each day of the year, that there is no way of locking You up, whether we realize it or not.

Thanks, Lord, for being in that manger, and thanks even more for not staying there!

Sen
sa
tion
al

DECEMBER 25 REVISITED

Lord, it's a few days after Christmas, and I'm afraid that many of us have already put You away with the rest of our Christmas decorations. Why do we do this to You? Why can't we see that You are a person, alive in us, and not merely a part of the Christmas formalities and trimmings?

We start at the manger each year, Lord, but it seems that too often we stop there. Help us to keep You in mind throughout the year. We really don't want to throw You out with the tree and tinsel.

Too often my Christmas joy freezes into apathy after I have read the Christmas cards I received. (Help me to at least think about and pray for some of the people I get cards from!)

Too often our holiday plans get in the way of You, and I get wrapped in the trappings and trapped in the wrappings.

Untangle me, Lord. Help get the tinsel out of my hair.

Refresh me with the gift of new birth in my life from You—each day of the year.

9. CHURCH

WHAT'S CHURCH?

I saw another "Peanuts" cartoon today, Lord.

It showed Charlie Brown trying to memorize his part in the Christmas Eve children's service. Lucy was right there heckling him, telling him he was going to forget his lines and blow the whole service.

Then we see Charlie walking out the door on his way to the service. Lucy is still there, shouting words of discouragement.

The next picture shows Charlie returning, coming in the front door, dejected and sad.

"You blew it, didn't you, Charlie Brown, didn't you? You forgot your lines, didn't you?" Lucy yells.

Charlie looks at her and says, "No, I forgot where the church was."

Lord, sometimes I forget where the church is too. Sometimes I am so busy trying to remember other things, or trying to use the right words, that I fail to see that Your church is not a building or a service but instead it is Your people, alive and involved in the world.

Help me be the church today, Lord. And don't let me forget where it is!

EOPLE PEOPLE PEOPLE PEOPLE PEO

GARAGE SALES, ANYONE?

Lord, I love the church; I really do.

I know You're still at work in and through it.

But sometimes I really get ticked off at all the things I see the church doing!

Lord, does Your church need to have flower shows, fashion shows, bake sales, car washes, knitting parties, lovely lunches, super suppers, big breakfasts? Maybe these events aren't all bad, but when such activities outnumber other things like study classes, exchange weekends, trips to the hospitals, worship opportunities, good fellowship opportunities without having to "make money," good discussion groups, then maybe the priorities are wrong.

Lord, show me and others that "Junk for Jesus" sales aren't the only way to serve You these days!

PEOPLE LIKE TO BE TREATED LIKE PEOPLE.

10. COMMUNION

CATCH A SMILE!

Lord, I smiled at Communion today!
I really did!

I was planning this for a long time. I was tired of seeing droopy droves of people march up and down the pews without even a hint of joy and celebration.

I was tired of wondering what people were thinking of me or if my hair was in place or if I would trip on the steps.

So, I think I did what was right, Lord. I smiled at people as I came from the Communion rail.

And it was great! Because some of the people smiled at me, Lord. And one elderly lady winked! And a 5-year-old even pointed at me!

Lord, wouldn't it be great if this type of smile were contagious? Let's pray for an epidemic!

II. CONFIRMATION

CONFIRMATION DAY

Well, Lord, it's over. Confirmation, that is. And I must say it's been quite a day—my first white robe, the new watch, all that money, and many friends around. But now what, Lord? Where do we go from here?

I made a pretty important vow to You today—I just hope I can keep it. But to be really honest, I don't think I'll be able to keep it. I want to be faithful to You every day, but I really goof things up—as You well know.

Live a little

Lord, at those times when I forget my vow to You and think only of myself, please remind me of my baptism in Your name. Two big vows have happened in my life—Your vow to me at my baptism and my vow to You on my confirmation day. Always let me remember that even though I may at times break my vow to You, Your promise to me at baptism is never broken. And let me remember that You have called me by name in my baptism, that You have marked me for life, and that my baptismal vow never expires. Lord, it's great to be confirmed; just let me always remember both my confirmation day and my baptism. And, Lord, I really did look pretty sharp in a white robe, didn't I?

12. DEATH

DEATH IS NOT AN "IN" WORD

Are most people afraid of death, Lord? To be honest, I'd have to say that I am at times too.

Death is a word I don't hear much about these days. When people have to talk about death, they usually refer to it as "passing away" or "leaving this world" or "being deceased." Why are people afraid to use the word "death," Lord?

And much of our society still tries to hide the reality of death, whether it's in the funeral home or in the family discussions or even in our churches. It's as if we were all afraid to talk about it because it might happen to us if we thought about death too much.

We need to think about death, don't we, Lord? And we can think about death in the right way because You have not only spoken about death but also done something about it—You've won over it! You've conquered death! And that *is* something to talk about!

Lord, when I die, I want the service to be a joyful celebration of life in the resurrection. I want people to be able to celebrate their life in You and also my death in You. I hope they sing a resurrection song of joy and help to remind one another that death, even though it's painful and humanly sorrowful, is also a time of joy because we know it is not the final event in life.

Lord, I worry about people who are afraid to die. I also worry about people that do not see a resurrection after death.

Help us to be able to talk about death more in our families and parishes. Help us to deal with it realistically because of the hope that You have given us in Your resurrection.

I feel better already, Lord, just in talking about it.

Help us to see that the sting is really gone forever!

THE DIFFERENCE BETWEEN LIFE AND DEATH

13. DOUBT

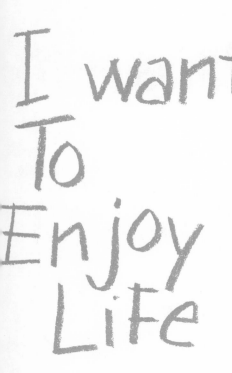

DOUBT IS A 5-LETTER WORD

Lord, I don't think the word doubt is such a bad word. Do You? I hear people saying that to doubt something is bad because it means I might not believe in it or that my faith is shaky if I doubt things.

But to be honest, Lord, I do doubt things. I doubt things about You and my faith. I doubt things that others seem to accept with no problem.

I'm kind of like Thomas in the Bible, Lord, because to me he was honest. He was having a hard time accepting You, and so he told others about it. That seems to be a better thing to do than not be able to share your real feelings with someone.

I like to call Thomas "honest" Thomas instead of "doubting" Thomas. His questions and concerns are real to me.

Lord, please stay with me in these times of doubt and concern. Please get me through these days of questioning my faith and my Lord. At this point You are still the only one I can turn to, even though I do have some questions regarding my faith and the Scriptures.

Help me to be honest and open, to be able to share my thoughts with others, so that You and Your people can build me up and set me straight.

I feel better already, Lord! Just call me another "honest" Thomas!

DO-IT-YOURSELF PRAYERS

14. EASTER

EASTER IS

Lord, we just had an Easter celebration in the basement of one of our youth members. Thirty teens were sitting all over the floor in grubby, casual clothes, talking and enjoying themselves. And this is what Easter meant to these kids (you know, the inexperienced, impulsive, revolutionary kind we read about!):

Easter is!
Because Christ lives—now, today!
So . . .
Sing!
Blow up a balloon!
Go fly a kite!
Shout hooray!
Kiss your neighbor!
Wave to a baby!
Paint your room orange and yellow!
Say hi to that grouch down the street!
Wear a "Happy" button!
Smile at the whole world!
Go buy a gift for someone.
And tell everybody—parents, teachers, friends—
that you love them!

It's Easter—and Easter is!
(That's something to cheer about!)

Hooray!

AN EASTER CHEER

Resurrection, Resurrection—Hooray!
Resurrection, Resurrection—Today!
It's hard to keep a good Man down.
Thanks for picking us up!
Help us to live it up! Today, Lord.

celebrate

15. ECOLOGY

ECOLOGY IS PICKING UP!

Lord, I'm glad to see that interest in ecology is picking up! I bet You are too!

But it seems it has become an "in" word that is losing its main significance already.

How can one company, for example, be interested in erasing pollution by selling one type of gas that lowers pollution but four other brands that increase pollution?

Who can really be against ecology, Lord? But I'm afraid that even the word "ecology" has become polluted.

CLEAN UP THE COUNTRY

16. FAILURE

LIVING ON THE RIGHT SIDE
OF THE RESURRECTION

Lord, I forgot again today. I forgot who I am and who You are. I seemed to fail in everything I tried.

I really got down today, Lord, because things just didn't go right. Everybody seemed to be against me. Nobody filled me up today. My friends seemed angry with me, my folks seemed to ignore me, and my teacher didn't even know I existed today.

Lord, when days like this happen, first give me enough courage and power to tell You about it. And then always remind me that the Resurrection has already happened. Remind me that after every Good Friday in my life Easter always comes.

Help me, Lord, to live on the right side of the Resurrection, not only on good days but each day of my life!

I think I'm going to make it, Lord! Thanks!

17. FAMILY

FAMILY COMMOTIONS

Lord, you know how we've tried to have family
    devotions at our house.
But it just doesn't work, does it?
Do other families have trouble like us?
Sometimes my dad can't get all of us together at
    the same time.
And sometimes he has to leave early for a meeting
    himself (even church meetings).
And sometimes our devotions seem kind of off-
    key and stiff.
I wish we could maybe just talk about some of the
    things that happen each day.
Maybe each of us could share the fun or the disap-
    pointments of the day and then let the rest
    of the family comment on them and help
    each other out.
Maybe we could all take turns saying a prayer at
    the end instead of using those old prayers
    out of our devotional book; or share Scrip-
    tural passages that recall things that hap-
    pened today.
And maybe if we start to share more of the real
    things in life, You too might be able to be-
    come more real to us.
Lord, change our family commotions into real
    devotions!

I LIKE HELPING PEOPLE TALK TO EACH OTHER

LIFE IS A LOT EASIER
IF YOU KNOW THE
FUNDAMENTALS

THE FAMILY
THAT LOVES TOGETHER . . . .

Thanks for my family, Lord! They're pretty important people to me.

Sure, we don't always see eye to eye, but I don't think we have to. A little "constructive conflict" at times helps to clear the air and adds to understanding.

Help me to accept my family members just as they are and not how I'd like them to be.

Help them to accept me just as I am, and I know that's not always easy.

And help us all to accept You as our living Lord who binds us together in love and forgiveness.

Help us to be "one for the other and all for You."

Thanks, Lord, it's great to be Your family!

18. FORGIVENESS

FORGIVENESS IS A PERSON

We've been fooled long enough, Lord. Forgiveness isn't a word that should be used only on Sunday mornings.
No, forgiveness is a person—a person who loves You and shares this love with me and others around him.

Let's get the word "forgiveness" out of the catechism and hymnbook and dictionary and into the lives and hands and voices of people—where it belongs.

Forgiveness is a person—starting with You, Lord!

SPEAKING THE LANGUAGE

19. GRADUATION

THE MOST VALUABLE GRADUATION PRESENT YOU'LL EVER GIVE COULD BE **you**

GRADUATION DAY

Well, Lord, here I am. I can't believe that I'm finally graduating!

I didn't think I'd make it, because it seemed so far away a few years ago. But now here I am. Me, a graduate!

And what now, Lord? Where do I go from here? It seems that so far my life has been pretty well laid out for me. I really haven't had too many big decisions to make. But now I do. Now I need to decide on the direction I want my life to take.

Help me, Lord, as I struggle for identity and purpose in this world. Help me to make the right decisions. Help me, not necessarily to be successful in all that I do, but do help me to be faithful in all that I do.

Graduation isn't the end of something, is it, Lord? It's not even the beginning. But it is more like a continuation of my constant life with You. And if I can keep this in mind, I know I won't be afraid.

Thanks, Lord, for the gift of Your presence each day. Thanks for seeing me through these long days of study. And thanks too for keeping with me.

And show me that graduation is not so much the time when I now must meet the "cruel, hard world" (that's what some people around me say, Lord), but rather graduation is another gift that You have given me as I continue my joy-filled life with You.

Bless those that have graduated with me too, Lord!

20. HUNGER

THE HUNGRY GIRL

I saw another picture of a hungry girl today, Lord,
in a magazine.
That makes about 10 of them this week.
I've also seen six pictures of kids playing in the
alleys and slums, three shots of Korean orphans,
and others showing the result of war and hatred
and injustice.
These pictures don't bother me, Lord—and that's
just the trouble!

I've seen so many of them that they have become
pictures, just plain horrible pictures, rather than
people crying out in need.

Lord, make these pictures become real to me. And
help me to make their hungry stomachs and torn
faces unreal to them.

HOW SWEET IT ISN'T

PRAYER PAGE — NOW IT'S YOUR TURN!

21. HYPOCRISY

WHAT DOES A HYPOCRITE LOOK LIKE?

Lord, what does a hypocrite look like? Does he look any different than an "ordinary, normal" person?

People say that there are a lot of hypocrites in the church today. But how do you pick them out? I tried it one Sunday and spent all my time looking and none of my time listening and worshiping.

Lord, even if there are these hypocrites around, maybe it would help if we'd stop looking for them so much and start sharing more of our faith and joy with others.

I can find things wrong with anybody and anything I want to if I look hard enough. But is that really our purpose in life, Lord, to find out all the bad things and complain about them?

I'd rather look at the good things and tell others how great they are because of You.

And who knows, maybe, just maybe those "hypocrites" might disappear in the process!

22. IDENTITY

I'M A ME . . . !

Lord, isn't it great that You made
only one of each of us!
I mean,
that's real planning.
And it also tells me a little more about You—
and me.

For example,
it tells me that You think I'm pretty important—
since there's only one of me around.
And it tells me that You must
expect some great things from me,
because You haven't made any substitutes for me.

It makes me feel kind of important, Lord; You know,
knowing that I just didn't happen but that You
made me as an individual.

Lord, let me be able to look at others
the way You look at me—as a person made by You
for purpose in life.

Don't let me look at people
only in groups or crowds,
but let me see each person as a person
distinctively different.

And please make my parents and teachers
and everyone else look at me as a Somebody
        and as a one-body.

It's great, Lord,
that there's only One of You too!

LABELS—FOR CANS ONLY!

Lord, why do I label people?

Why do I pass judgment on people
before I really get to know them?
I know many people do it, Lord.
Like the lady who doesn't like that boy
because of the length of his hair;
or the youth who thinks his neighbor
is a "stuffed shirt"
even though they have never talked together;
or the fella who thinks another person
is mad at him
because she didn't smile at him once.

Help me to stop labeling people
before I get to understand them.
Don't let me stereotype people
or assume something about them
that might not be true.
You can help me do this, Lord, because You have
already labeled me at my baptism, when You called
me "Your own." You have labeled all of us as "forgiven," "loved," and "worthy" because of Your
death and resurrection.

Then let me reach out to others to really get to
know them instead of merely putting a handy label
on them.

Thanks, Lord, for labeling me as one of Yours.
Now free me to get to know people as they are. And
make me take the time to be "a people" to others
too.

23. INCIDENTALS Life goes by

LITTLE THINGS MEAN A LOT

Lord, today I'd like to thank You for the small things in life. I thank You for them because they mean a lot to me.

I forget about small things in life, Lord. I'm so busy looking at the big things that I just walk over the incidentals. But when I stop to think of it, it's the small things that add much to my life.

Lord, thanks for such things as:

the sidewalk that keeps my feet out of the mud,
the pen I use that writes most of the time
the man at the 7-11 store that happily sells me milk,
clean clothes that always seem to find their way
     into my dresser,
the lady that makes sure I have clean clothes in my
     dresser,
the 10:00 p. m. newsman that keeps me up with the
     latest,
the church custodian that keeps the church
     grounds looking sharp,
the little sparrow that sits outside on the back
     fence,
the neighbor's little baby that always has a smile,
the farmers out west somewhere who make sure
     I have my bowl of cereal each morning,
and the chicken who works hard so I have a com-
     plete breakfast,
the men who deliver the mail, even the ones that
     bring the bills,
the friendly telephone ladies who try to assist me
     on a misdialed call,

the nurse who works the night shift in case I need
to use the emergency room,
the grass that makes the yard look nice, even
though I have to cut it,
and the many people in my daily life that do little
things for me
without which I could not enjoy the life You have
given me!

Thanks, Lord, for the little things in life. They really
are kind of big!

so fast. Stop for a moment

and take a look at it.

24. LAUGHTER

LAUGH AND LIVE IT UP!

I like people who laugh a lot, Lord. They're fun to be around.

People who laugh a lot seem to have many things going for them. They seem to get more out of life; they seem to enjoy every phase of it.

Teach people to laugh again, Lord. So many of us have forgotten. We've looked at our problems and worries without first looking at You.

Brighten up faces again, Lord. Make people show their teeth.

You have the power, Lord, to start people —

rolling in the aisles,
laughing at each other,
getting a side ache
laughing at themselves.

Make me someone that others want to be around because I am happy and laugh a lot.

I'm happy, Lord, and I want to tell others too!

(HA-HA-HA, HOORAY ME)

We sell fun

58

25. LIFE

GOD IS GREAT; GOD IS GOOD: AND WE THANK HIM FOR OUR—LIFE!

What is this thing called LIFE, Lord? We call You the Lord of life—okay, what's it all about?

One day I'm really on top of things; the next day I could care less. One day life is great, and I shout a big, "Hooray"! The next day I won't even lift my head to say boo. I like to live, Lord, but I'm kind of afraid to live—You know, really say what I want to say and feel and express myself.

I know real life is found in You, but I sure wish a few more adults and kids would share this joy in life with me instead of hiding it
or talking about it
or being afraid to smile.

Lord, let me enjoy life, really live it! Let me say "hooray" to life to others too! And please pick me up when I'm down. And let me pick others up too!

Don't let me blame You for things either—that sure is easy. When I have problems or goof things up, it sure is easy to get down on You. Don't let me put hurts in the driver's seat; let me keep my eye on You!

I've got to go now. I need to get on living. And living means keeping in touch with You and sharing You with others!

HOORAY for life!

Lord, thanks for making life more than a magazine!

A BOY WHO LOST AN EYE

Lord, I'm really down today because I heard that a good friend of mine had lost an eye in a senseless accident. He was walking home from school and was shot by a pellet-type gun. There was no way to save the eye.

I'm sorry, Lord, but this one is hard for me to accept. The big WHY keeps coming to my mind.

Lord, first of all, help Tom accept this great loss in the best way You can.

Then, Lord, help me and Tom's other friends to be able to accept the whole situation also. We need You to show us that life still goes on after a thing like this has happened.

And help me to use the right words when I talk to Tom. Maybe the best thing You can show me is not what words to say, because words are too easy, but instead show me how to just be a person to him, a person who cares and accepts him as he is.

And there's a lesson in all of this too, isn't there Lord? Maybe this is Your lesson to me for the day. You have opened all of our eyes in a spiritual way by coming to die and live for us. Our eyes can "see" what life is all about through You.

Nothing can take this type of "sight" from any of us. Lord, help Tom and me too to "see" You through the people around us.

And knowing Tom, maybe his "sight" is better than most of ours as he accepts life as a gift and thanks You for both kinds of sight that he still has.

BE SENSE-ABLE

Lord, I was reading where people learn
        1% through taste,
        1.5% through touch,
        3.5% through smell,
        11% through hearing, and
        83% through sight.

Lord, make all my senses in some way tell me of Your presence and love for me—even when my nose is stuffed up, my taste is dull, my hearing is slight, my sight is blurred.

Let me ''sense'' You in all of life, Lord! That makes sense!

THAT ONE WISH

Lord, if you would grant me just one wish, you know what it would be?

I would wish that there would be peace on earth among all people. Now, wait a minute. I think first I would rather ask for all the hungry people to be fed. But on second thought I would like people to better understand other people. No, now I want to change my wish so that no one would have to live in poverty anymore.

Lord, I don't know what my one wish would be. You're either going to have to give me more than one wish — or else that one wish of mine should be wisdom to do what You want me to do on this earth!

PRAYER PAGE—
LORD I WANT TO TALK TO YOU

EXPECT THE IMPOSSIBLE!

Lord, today is going to be a rough one—and I am a little scared of what will happen.

Lord, today assure me that in a world where even carpenters are resurrected anything is possible!

ONE OF THE
NOBLEST THINGS
A MAN CAN DO
IS DO THE BEST
HE CAN

26. LONELINESS

LONELINESS

Lord, I heard a person today say that he was ugly, clumsy, and stupid and no one likes him. I heard a person say that no one cares about him. Everyone laughs at him, he has no friends. I heard a person say that no one needs him, that no one cares if he lives or dies. I heard a person say that he's going to solve everyone's problems, that he might just end it all right now, today. I heard a person say that he did not want to live anymore and that he was ready to give up on life—until he went home and saw his little puppy staring up at him with those big, soft, loving, dark-brown eyes!

Lord, help me to share my love with those who are lonely and afraid of love. And help people to see that Your love is much deeper and stronger than puppy love!

27. LOVE

SAY IT TOO!

Lord, there are so many ways that You say, "I love you," to me each day—through friends and food and good weather and forgiveness and life itself.

Help me today, Lord, to also say, "I love You," to You and to people that need to hear the words— my folks, my neighbor, my pastor, my teacher, and even my little brother.

I need to hear those words from You, Lord.

Help me to see that others also need to hear those words from me!

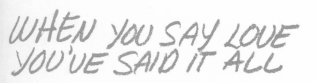

WHEN YOU SAY LOVE
YOU'VE SAID IT ALL

28. MONEY

HAPPY MONEY

Lord, this month our congregation is having stewardship meetings. It's the annual push to try to get people thinking about their gifts and how to share Your blessings with others.

A highlight of the evenings is a little skit which our youth are doing, called "Happy Money." In it they accuse people of giving sad money to God.

This really hits home, Lord. It's so easy to give only half generously, thinking of all the "better" ways to spend Your money.

Lord, help us all to give happy money to You. Help us to accept all of life as a gift from You, and then help us to be able to give back to You in an exciting way these gifts in order that others might grow in Your love too.

Money is happy or sad, depending on how it's used.

Keep giving us the power to give happy money, Lord!

Splurge
(a little)

29. MORNING

THE GIFT OF TODAY

Lord, I'm having a good day today.
Yesterday I was kinda down,
but today I'm with it again.
I feel good, but I'm not sure why.
Maybe it's because the group chuckled a little
when I told that joke.
Maybe it's because I feel people
have been recognizing me a little today.
And maybe it's because
I feel worth something today—
that life has meaning.
Help me, Lord, to be worth something to people;
and help me to help people find their worth also.
Thanks, Lord, for picking me up
and letting me fly today.
And try to make tomorrow a good day too!

Make Morning

A QUICK PRAYER FOR THE MORNING

Another day—I wonder what kind of a day it will
be! Much depends on me, Lord, what I want to
get out of this day and what I want to put into this
day.
Start me off on the right foot, Lord.
Let me be sensitive to the people around me, Lord.
And remind me that You will be with me
throughout the day; show me my baptism.
With that taken care of, Lord, I'll do the rest.
Look out, world, here I come!

the
Last

A Special M

EVERY NIGHT AT THE MOVIES

Lord, what do You think of the movies of today? Do You rate them GP, R, X, or Z? I guess it depends on what one wants a movie to do.

Some statistics show that a 17-year-old has seen over 500 films in his life. I don't know who counted, but, regardless, that's a lot of movies. Even if the figure is off by 100 or more!

Movies of today are a powerful force in people's lives, both in the good sense and in the bad sense.

I like movies too, Lord, but it's almost getting to the point that movies are becoming more "true to life" than life itself! And that's a little frightening.

There are a lot of religious films out today too, and I don't mean the big spectaculars like "King of Kings" and "Lord of Lords." Some of those biggies seem less religious than some of the other message films around.

Lord, keep speaking through movies that we see. And keep my mind open as I view the good ones and the not-so-good ones. Help films show me that You exist in people; help films show me that Your love speaks to the many problems in this world; help films show me of the destruction that sin still makes in the world; help films show me how to enjoy life to its fullest.

Help me to be able to laugh at some of the films too, Lord. Don't let us take life too seriously all of the time and lose the excitement and joy that You still put into it.

And, Lord, don't let me be suckered into films by sneaky adults who make the films. Help me to realize that the advertisements for any film are not as good (or as bad) as the film itself.

And help me to see You in all of life—in living color —whether or not I'm accompanied by an adult!

PRIORITY PRAYERS

31. NEW YEAR

HAPPY NEW YEAR

It's another year, Lord. Thanks for the blessings and guidance during the past year. Not everything went the way I had planned, but I do know that You were with me every day and hour of the year.

A new year is not that exciting to me, Lord. Oh, sure, I enjoy the holiday break, the change of pace, the parties, the days off from school. And it is a good time to reevaluate myself and to ask where I am going and where I have been. It's too bad that some people aren't able to change more of their life each year as they see their shortcomings and failures. The only thing most people change is the date on the letters and school assignments. And for some it takes until April to get the year right.

Help me, Lord, to accept this new year as a gift from You. Help me to look back to see my failures and frustrations and then help me to see that they are all forgiven. And help me to see that this forgiveness happens every day with You, not just at the end of the year.

I'm glad, Lord, that my relationship to You is in the shape of a straight line and not a circle. In other words, I'm glad that Your love for me is always there, instead of me having to renew it each year like a car license or activity card.

Help me to be alive to You and the people around me this year. Help me to see that maybe this world does not need more resolutions in Your name but more revolutions in Your name!

Happy New Year, in Your name! Amen.

32. OCCUPATION

PUT "CARE" IN YOUR CAREER!

Lord, if anyone else asks me, "What are you going to be when you grow up?" I'm going to scream!

I'm not sure yet what I want to do or be. And I guess I already know what I am—a person loved by You. But for many people around me that's not enough.

Lord, as I seek to decide on a lifework, keep me mindful that I will become nothing more than what I already am. And as I choose a profession, let me select one that helps me to serve people. Keep people as a priority in my life.

Put CARE in my career!

HELP

THE WORLD WOULD BE A BETTER PLACE

33. PEOPLE

PEOPLE PRESENT—
HANDLE WITH CARE!

Lord, thanks for the people that You put in my life today. People are the greatest gifts You give.

I don't understand some people when they say they need to get away sometimes into the mountains and wilderness in order to commune better with You. It seems to me that's one way of copping out.

Because You come to me through people, Lord, right? I know mountains and hills are Your doings also, but I think we need to see You more in people —people hurting and in need throughout the world.

Help us to handle people with care, Lord. Help us to see that it is in people where You dwell also, not just in the quiet countryside.

Send us, Lord, not only where the action is but also where the hurting is.

Help us handle people with care, Lord, because You are present in the faces around us.

How would you like a nice little gift?

LET'S HEAR IT FOR OUR FRIENDS

Today I'd like to pray for my friends. Bless them real good, okay?

I pray for them because it's so easy to take them for granted. Keep me mindful of their needs too.

I pray for them because they are my friends. It's kind of great that they know me through and through—and still accept me as their friend!

Bless, guide, and power them, Lord, to be Your people as they share joy and excitement with me.

I have great friends, Jesus. And that's with a capital "F" too!

SNAP THE GAP

I know kids who don't like their folks; I know adults who don't like their kids.

I know teachers who can't stand students; I know students who can't stand teachers.

I know neighbors who have never talked to each other.

I know families that never talk to each other.

Lord, help me be a small part in showing people that You have already snapped every gap that ever existed, if people would only see You in others.

Lord, help me be a bridge between You and other people.

Lord, snap the gap in my own life!

CHARLIE BROWN THEOLOGY

Lord, maybe Charlie Brown is right when he says he loves mankind, but it's people he can't stand.

Because I can love people in general more than I can individually.

Lord, it's like the joke about the father who yelled at his kids when they walked in the wet cement of his sidewalk: he can love them in the abstract but never in the concrete.

Lord, I like people, but there are a number of them that really get to me.

I know I should love them, but certain kinds of people just turn me sour.

Like the guy that keeps wanting help with his schoolwork or the girl who tells everyone I like her or the relative who still treats me like a 5-year-old when I was "only that high."

I need patience and help, Lord.

Maybe I need to see a little more of You in them.

And maybe I need to see a little more of You in me.

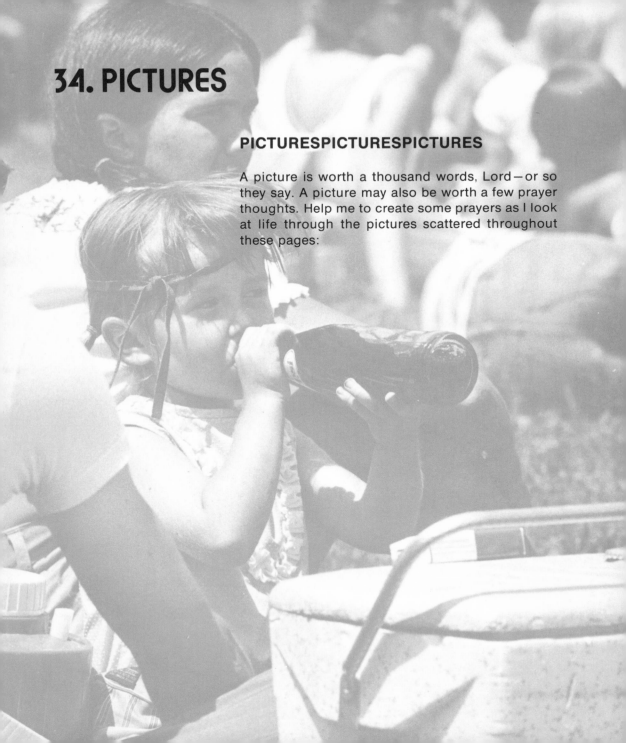

34. PICTURES

PICTURESPICTURESPICTURES

A picture is worth a thousand words, Lord — or so they say. A picture may also be worth a few prayer thoughts. Help me to create some prayers as I look at life through the pictures scattered throughout these pages:

PRAYER PAGE—IT'S FREE!

35. POLITICS

take the trouble

A PRAYER FOR POLITICIANS

Lord, I must say at the start that if there's one profession that has a bad reputation, it's politics. And that's a bad situation if you ask me! (I know You didn't ask me, but I thought I'd share that anyway.)

Lord, rather than having people look suspiciously at politicians, why don't more of our good-type citizens enter this field? People in politics are no better or worse than any other profession. But it is sad that so many politicians who are trying to do a good job are ridiculed because of a few.

Help us to pray for our politicians, Lord. Help us to help them do the best job they can. Help us to look positively on their great responsibilities. And help us to change the image we have given them.

And while we're praying, Lord, maybe we can also get some action going. Maybe we can write our congressman and give him a vote of confidence. Maybe we can volunteer to work for our local mayor. Maybe we can consider taking an active role in government ourselves.

We have the power to change the image of the politician, Lord. And in so doing we might also change some of the priorities and views of the men that are in these positions.

We really do have power to change a lot of things, Lord. Just help us to realize this, and power us to encourage and enable those in various offices to do the best job they can as they keep people as priorities!

Help us to make the earthly kingdoms a little more heavenly, Lord!

36. POPCORN

THANKS FOR POPCORN, LORD!

Lord, I'd like to thank You for popcorn! That's right — nice, ordinary, salted, hot-buttered popcorn.

I bet a lot of us popcorn-lovers forget to thank You for such trivial things as popcorn. So this prayer is dedicated to trivial things like popcorn.

What would a movie be without popcorn? What would a slumber party be without popcorn? How exciting would a circus be without popcorn? And what would the animals at the zoo do without popcorn?

So thanks for popcorn, Lord! If You think enough of us to give us popcorn, You must think enough of us to give us the essential needs too.

I pray that I always think enough of You to thank You for popcorn!

37. PRAYER

HOW LONG IS A PRAYER?

Lord, how long should a prayer be?

Do you really like long prayers, Lord? How long does a prayer have to be for it to "take"?

I don't like long, drawn-out prayers to You.
I like the quick openers that come right to the point. In a church service, Lord, is it really necessary to tell You that Grandma Schultz, who is the mother of Mrs. Smith, is in Room 103 of Memorial Hospital and would like to be visited after 3 p.m. on Monday?

Lord, maybe we mix up what a prayer is and instead make it into a general announcement.

Help me, Lord, either to accept long prayers or else to tell the pray-er to shorten them.

I think the Lord's Prayer is about the right length.

I better stop now; this prayer is getting too long.

THINK ABOUT IT

A PRAYER WHEN YOU HAVE NOTHING TO PRAY ABOUT

I wonder if I'm the only one, Lord, who sometimes has nothing to pray about. Oh, I'm sure I could think of some things, but right now I just feel like enjoying some of the things You have given me today—like good health, a clean and bright shirt, a sunny day, a friend's smile, a good peanut butter-and-jelly sandwich, and on and on and on. (Come to think of it, Lord, maybe I am praying to You when I use the gifts that You give me each day!)

make the best

PRAYER IS NOT AN IBM COMPUTER

When should I pray, Lord? I know that's a simple question, but it seems I'm in a rut.

Sure, You know I pray before every meal (well, almost all of them) and every night when I go to bed. But should prayer be a routine thing?

I have made prayers a ritual. I have programed them to happen only at certain times of the day. You must really be swamped with prayers at mealtime and bedtime, Lord!

Lord, help me to remember to pray at other times of my life. Help me to pray—

> when I get a new pair of shoes,
> when I see a great TV special,
> when I meet a new friend,
> when I see a flower,
> when I'm driving to the store.

Make prayer happen in my life throughout the day, not only when I'm hungry or going to bed.

Make my prayer life spontaneous, not programed; unusual, not commonplace; exciting, not routine.

And thanks, Lord, for the time it has taken to pray to You right now!

of a good thing

NOTHING LEFT BUT PRAYER!

Lord, I just heard a fellow say, "Well, I guess there's nothing to do now but to pray."

If I were You, I would take that as an insult. The nerve of someone saying that he has tried everything else so now he might as well try praying, since nothing else worked.

Lord, why can't people see that prayer is doing something—something very important? Why do so many people fail to see the power of prayer? Why is prayer listed on the bottom of our priorities rather than at the top?

I heard someone else the other day state that prayer is more important than eating. I wonder if many people forgot to eat today, Lord?

PRAYERS OF PRAISE!

in thy name we pray

WHAT SHOULD WE CALL YOU, LORD?

Are You God or Jesus or Spirit or heavenly Father?

I'm confused, Lord, because I hear people praying to You by calling You different names. And even in the same prayer!

They start a prayer with "Dear heavenly Father," call You "Spirit" ten words later, and end up with "in Thy name, Jesus."

I'm confused because I really don't know how to address You. Or does it really matter?

Lord, help me to keep Your name right.
Don't let me mix up Your names.
Keep me straight.

And keep me aware, too, Lord, that even though we do get our human words crossed and confused, You still do listen and hear our words, mixed and confused though they be.

Thanks, Lord, Jesus, Spirit, Savior, God!

IN THY NAME WE PRAY!

38. PRIORITIES

KEEP OUR PRIORITIES STRAIGHT, LORD!

Lord, I need You to straighten out my priorities. I seem to put so much time and effort in "little" things that I forget about the "bigger" things in life.

Like I spend so much time worrying about things that I have no control over anyway. Or it seems that I try to use people to get my own way rather than loving them like You do. I change the phrase "Love people—use things" around and "Love things and use people."

My priorities in life need an overhaul, Lord. And it has to start with putting You in first place. You're either in first place in a person's life or no place at all. And I'm trying, Lord, I really am.

Fill me with Your power and patience. Keep me loving people and using things. And while you're at it, Lord, help our country to keep her priorities straight too. We spend more on food for dogs and cats than we do on food for the hungry. We spend more money on advertisements than we do on education. Something's wrong someplace, Lord.

You're Number One, Lord. Help me to show it in my daily life.

39. PROBLEMS

BOY, DO WE HAVE PROBLEMS!

Lord, there really are a lot of problems around, aren't there? I just can't wait to get to heaven to see how people live without problems. I just can't imagine how that will be. But I know it'll be great!

I just looked at the front page of the paper, and all I see are problems:—bank holdup, car accident, war, robbery, rape. Even the weather picture looks bad!

Do I have more problems than most people, Lord? I really don't know how one tells, but maybe that's not the important thing. Maybe the key is in how we look at life.

Problems can really get me down, Lord, because they are so real. And maybe some of my worries are little by other people's standards, but they sure are big to me.

It's like the story of the man who felt sorry for himself because he had no shoes but then didn't feel so bad when he saw another man who had no feet.

Lord, help me to have the right attitude towards life. Help me to see that You didn't promise me a rose garden. Even if You did, You also said there would be plenty of thorns in it!

Let me look to You as the source of power and comfort when problems hit. Let me remember my baptism each day and remember that You are with me, no matter what. And that's great news!

Help me to be like another man I heard about the other day. He was wearing one shoe, and another man said, "Say, did you lose a shoe?" And the first fella said, "No, I just found one!" It all depends on how we look at life.

Thanks, Lord, for being You. Help me to look past my problems to see You in all of life. Let me first look through the cross and the empty tomb and then see my problems in this perspective.

Me, a problem? What problem? Thanks, Lord!

40. RESPECT

DON'T KNOCK IT TILL YOU'VE TRIED IT

RESPECT BEGINS WITH ME

Lord, many people have lost respect for others in this world; what are we going to do about it?

Many youth have lost respect for adults; many adults have lost respect for youth. Many blacks have lost respect for whites; many whites have lost respect for blacks. And on and on and on.

Lord, help us to accept each other more as people, Your people. Help us to respect people just because they are people, Your people.

Lord, don't allow moms and dads to teach their children to respect only the policeman but also the garbageman. Don't let me respect only those I agree with; but also show me how to respect all people—because they are people.

Unconditional respect—that's what we need! We need to respect people not because they are special to us, but we first need to respect people because they are people to us.

Help me to see that all people are worthy of respect —the policeman, the teacher, the senior citizen, the teeny-bopper, the garbageman—not because of what they are but because of who they are!

And let respect start with me, Lord!

41. RESPONSE-ABILITY

THE ABILITY TO RESPOND

Lord, how does one get responsibility? Who gives it? Where can I find some?

People accuse young people of not being responsible. Perhaps there's some truth in it, but to generalize is wrong. And doesn't responsibility have to be learned—from adults and those around you?

I try to act responsible, but I know I flub up quite often. I don't want to, but it does happen. When I do, I wish those around me would pick me up and show me the right way and not lose faith in me.

And I think there's more to this word "responsible" than meets the eye. Because of You, Lord, all of Your people are response-able; we are capable of responding to others' needs because of what You have done for us. The potential is there—now we just need time and a chance to respond!

This also says, then, that all people, young and old, are capable of ministering to one another, that I don't have to wait to be over 21 in order to be a response-able Christian. My baptism gives me the power right now.

Lord, today help me to share my response-ability with those around me. And watch their eyes light up when I show them my newfound power!

What a great way to live! Thanks, Lord!

if you don't
do it yourself,
it won't get done

42. SCHOOL

MEANWHILE, BACK IN MY ALGEBRA CLASS. . . .

Here I am, Lord, sitting in my algebra class.
Did you ever have to take math, Lord?
"2B or not 2B" is the big question for the day.

And while I sit here, dreaming about figures and equations, I can't help thinking of the lonely lady sitting in the old folks' home with no one to talk to; or the little boy playing in the dirty alley with no one there to play catch with him; or the hundreds of people I could be talking to and helping out and pepping up today, instead of sitting here, with my pencil and paper, trying to figure out if "2Y plus 3X really equals 72."

And by the way, Lord, help me to remember that all those lonely people will still be lonely, even after algebra is over!

5 ITEMS FOR MY PRAYER LIST TODAY

ARE WE MAKING
THE GRADE WITH YOU?

What are school grades, Lord? How important are they in Your life?

In my life they are very important. I need good grades to continue my education, to be eligible for school organizations and the football team. My parents demand that I bring home nothing worse than a *B.* I am ranked according to my grade-point average.

Sometimes I think grades are really overdone. I have even been tempted to cheat, just so I can keep up with my grades. Too many people put too much emphasis on them. Right now I may not be getting a very good education, but I sure am getting good grades!

Do You grade me too, Lord, each day? Did I fail yesterday because I was in a horrible mood? Or what about last Wednesday when I lost my temper at my dad?

Do You have a grading system something like this:

I get an *A* for helping a grandma across the street.
I get a *B* if I take the garbage out.
I get a *C* if I forget to clean my room sometimes.
I get a *D* if I come in late from a date.
I get an *F* if I don't do anything worthwhile some day.

I can't believe that You would fail anyone, Lord. That's what my faith tells me. I mean, how does a person fail life?

Lord, help me to do two things: Help me to keep grades in the right perspective. Help others too. And also help me to see that Your love for me is always A+. That You always look at me as Your "favorite pupil." That You look at everyone that way.

There are people around me that look like they have failed life. Let me "bring up their grade" by showing them concern and forgiveness.

Lord, with You I've made the grade. Because You have given Your life for me so that I can have real life now.

In Your class, Lord, everyone receives an A, not because of their achievement but because of the work their Teacher has done for them.

Education

College

DO YOU HAVE TO GO TO COLLEGE TO GO TO HEAVEN?

Lord, why does everyone assume that after a person graduates from high school he automatically goes to college?

Why do they keep asking me, "What college do you go to?" Is it a sin not to go these days, Lord? Do you have to go to college to succeed?

Please, Lord, help people to see that doing something besides going to college is not a decision worse than death. Help people not to label kids as "dropouts" just because at this time in their life they have chosen to do something other than go the college route.

Sure, school is important, but it is also important to have other options. And help people to see too that the sheepskin is not the main thing in life, but of primary importance is seeing You as the Shepherd of all of life.

Did you go to college, Jesus?

43. SONGS

HYMN 200

That's my favorite hymn, Lord.
I don't really like all of the songs in our hymnbook;
some are too slow, others too sad, some have
strange words, others are too high.
But in Hymn 200, Lord, You really reach me!
Because we sing, "I know that my Redeemer lives!"
You know why I like that?
Because that's the summary of my faith!
Notice we don't sing, "I think that my Redeemer
lives,"
> or, "I sure hope that my Redeemer lives,"
> or, "It sure would be nice if my Redeemer
> lives."
No, we sing, "I know that You live!"
And that's something to sing about!
Don't let them change that song, Lord!

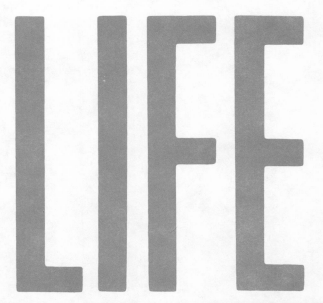

SING A SONG OF JOY!

I know a guy who sings all day long, Lord!
It used to bug me because I couldn't figure out how
anyone could be happy all the time.
But now I know why. He loves life!

He sings all types of songs—
        "top 40" tunes,
        hymnbook types,
        all types.
And it's great.

A popular poster says, "Everyone has something
to sing about." And that's pretty theological, isn't
it, Lord, if we keep You in mind each day.

Help me to share some "Son-shine" too, Lord,
even if my voice isn't as good as Wilbur's. Help
me to sing and hum and sing again for the joy that
is mine today!

Yes, Lord, even a song is a sign of love!

44. SPORTS

A PRAYER FOR THE PIGSKIN

Lord, why do you let people pray at football games? I mean, it sometimes seems like a big fake when the student-body president gets up and prays that he hopes no one is hurt and that it is a fair game — and then after the prayer he joins in with the rest of the crowd that shouts, "Kill 'em, kill 'em!"

And why do you let some teams pray after the game? It sometimes looks like the coaches are trying to use prayer to settle their players down, to squelch tempers, to stop fistfights.
Now maybe that's okay, but it seems to me that prayer has to be more than that.

Wouldn't it be great to have a prayer at a football game and pray for:
the groundsmen who made the field so nice and neat before the game?
the neighbor next to the stadium who gets irritated at the noise every Friday night?
the freshman who didn't go to the game because he is a loner and no one would go with him? and even the hardworking ladies who popped all the stale popcorn?
And maybe we could even mention the pig, without whose skin the game could never be played.

Lord, I've changed my mind — allow us to keep praying at football games and wherever we are — only change the intent of some of our prayers!

101

45. SUMMER

IT'S SUMMER

SUMMERTIME

Summertime can be either great or terrible, Lord.

Summertime can be fun because I have more time to do things. But summertime can also become a drag because I have nothing to do.

Summertime is one of my favorite times, Lord. I'm glad You made it! But along with the joys of summer come the problems of summer:

Where can I find a job?

Why does Mom think I should do so much around the house?

What can I do today?

Why can't we go on vacation like everybody else?

I wish school would start again!

Lord, summer is a great time to do things for other people. It's a time when I need to give more of my time to others. There are people lonely and sad and hurting all over my town. Maybe You've given me so much time this summer in order to give my time to others.

Lord, lead me to the old folks' home so I can visit with the lonely; lead me to my neighbors who need an ear to talk to; help me to volunteer my time and energies to people this summer, so that summertime can be fun for them too. And it might even be more fun for me.

Thanks for the summer, Lord. Now let me use it wisely!

PRAYER PAGE – BE CREATIVE!

46. WAR AND PEACE

THE WORLD SCENE

Lord, two of the most-often-heard words these days are "peace" and "war." Was it that way in Your day too?

Peace and war mean so many things to so many people that they've lost a lot of their meaning. They have become "argument" words because of the definitions they've taken.

Just about everyone is for peace and against war, Lord, but that's as far as it goes. Some think that in order for there to be peace we have to have war.

I think we have misused Your Word so often in this respect, Lord. We have turned Your Bible into a weapon against each other. Both sides, the hawks and the doves, can prove their views from the same Book.

I have a side too, Lord. And I feel it's Your side. Like, what did You mean by "peacemaker" except a maker of peace? And what is all Your talk about love about if it doesn't start with others? And I always thought You wanted us to take seriously the passage, "He that loses his life for My sake will find it."

Lord, help us to find real peace in You. Help us to understand the other side too. But make us holy people that care about other people instead of seeing the other side as statistics.

And maybe the word "dove" has more significance for us than many people realize.

Send us Your peace-filled Spirit. Soon, Lord, soon!

47. WORDS

WORDS, WORDS, WORDS, WORDS, WORDS, WORDS

Lord, do we always have to use words to pray to You?

Help us to see that we don't always have to verbalize our thoughts.

Following is my own kind of prayer without the use of words. I know You'll accept this kind too.

MY PRAYER
(Use your own prayer thoughts to pray this one)

48. WORLD

COME AND SEE THE WORLD!

Lord, You have made a beautiful world. The only problem is that I feel a lot of people are looking right past it!

Your world is good, Lord. I hear so many people saying just the opposite. I hear them saying that the world is bad and that I must be afraid of the world. I'd like to think that the world is good because You made it and that You want me to enjoy it as much as possible.

Maybe it's a problem in terminology. I know, Lord, that sin is all over Your great world. But to me You have already taken care of sin and evil. Sure, it's still around, but You are bigger and more powerful than all the sin put together.

Maybe if more people would see Your world as Your world, given to us out of love to use and enjoy, then the big emphasis on sin and evil would fade a little more into the background. At least that's a nice thought, isn't it?

Lord, thanks for Your world. For all the things I see and forget to see. For all the big things and the little things. For things such as:

a squirrel
a leaf
a mailbox
a kangaroo
a refrigerator
a star
a dandelion

the daily newspaper
my neighbor
his dog
for colors
and lights
and weeds
and rain
and even the bugs that we try to get rid of.

This is Your world, Lord. I know You are still active
and alive in it.

And I'm glad!

49. WORSHIP

DELIVER US FROM LITANIES, O LORD!

Lord, I have a confession to make.
I am sorry, but I get lost in all the words of some of the litanies we pray in church.
These words might mean a lot to the writer of them, but they mean so little to me who stumbles through them.

I feel embarrassed and uncomfortable too by merely repeating the big words which I really don't understand. How do you "beseech" someone anyhow, Lord?

It doesn't help me either with the man in front of me mumbling some words and the girl next to me being uninspired by the mouthing of other's words.

Deliver me, Lord, from never-ending litanies, for they get in my way of honest and individual worship of You.

And also, Lord, keep reminding me that You can speak to us through thoughts and actions and, yes, even long litanies that I do not like!

We have a hap

THE PALM SUNDAY CHRISTIAN

There are lots of Palm Sunday Christians running around, Lord. You know, the guys who make Palm Sunday a kind of Calm Sunday and see Your march to the cross as simply a nice weekend parade, and everybody loves a parade, you know.

It's still easy in these days to see You coming into our city, as You did at Jerusalem, in order to give us a good life, healthier air, nicer neighbors, a better community, rather than seeing that Your presence in us makes us able to die in ourselves in order to be resurrected in You.

To believe in You, Lord, as someone has said, is to be able to die and not be embarrassed.

Lord, don't let us "palm" off our responsibilities of being called Your people. Help us to share Your death and resurrection with those around us. We all love a parade, Lord; just make it for the right reason.

by solution

PRAYERS FOR PEOPLE
THAT NEED PRAYERS

TRUE CONFESSIONS

Lord, I confess to You that there are often times
that I don't feel like confessing to You.
Sometimes in a worship service, when I'm sup-
posed to feel sorry for my sins or feel bad and
unworthy, I really don't feel bad at all.

Is that bad, Lord? Because sometimes during
confession I really feel great because I know all
my sins have been erased, and I just can't make
myself feel bad about that!
Forgive me, Lord, for feeling forgiven!
And help me, Lord, to act forgiven to others!

Look on the light side

A LIGHT THOUGHT

Who started the ritual of acolytes, Lord? It's really quite an interesting part of the service. And it might even rank as the number-one interest-maker for the entire hour.

The poor acolyte, realizing that he's being watched by "thousands" of eyes—his mom is praying that he doesn't trip on his nicely pressed robe; his grandma is hoping that he doesn't knock down the last candle; the preacher is wishing that he'd hurry up and get them doused so the service can end; the organist is sweating it out in hopes that her music will end at the exact time when the last candle goes out; and the acolyte might be wondering how he ever got into this situation.

I've noticed that the little children really enjoy this part of the service, Lord. Not only because it's at the end but because there's action in it.

Lord, maybe the best part of the acolyte ritual is that it is the part of the service that brings all of the people together. Everyone wants the acolyte to do a good job. Everyone is together in the body, silently cheering him on. And that's kind of Christian, isn't it?

I know, Lord, that maybe I should be praying to myself instead of watching the acolyte so much. But it is possible to pray to You while rooting for another successful accomplishment, isn't it?

Assure me, Lord, that even if the acoylte fails to light one of the candles some Sunday morning, the service is still valid and good. Don't let any ritual get in the way of joyful worship of You.

50. YOUTH

POOF—NO MORE TEEN-AGERS!

Lord, why don't You teach all the adults in the world a big lesson today—why don't You hide all of the teen-agers for just one day?

Can you just imagine what would happen if there were no teens in the whole world?

Who would all the magazines write about if there were no kids drinking, dragging, or drugging?

Who would go to the dirty movies that the adults produce?

Who would shoplift all those items that kids are accused of taking?

And who would mark up all the desks in the schools?

Lord, I don't mean to deny that kids get into trouble. But it does bother me when youth are classified and stereotyped as all bad and all dangerous and all wild. Was it the same way when You were a teen-ager, Lord?

Lord, help people, young and old, to look at one another as people, as individuals.

Let adults know that there is no such thing as a "typical teen-ager."

And let youth know that not all of the "over-30 variety" are stupid and unconcerned.

Don't let adults respect youth just because they are youth.

But also, don't let adults disrespect youth just because they are youth.

113

If only everyone would look at people
        the way You do, Lord!
And let Your kind of "looking" begin with me!

And maybe You better forget about hiding all those
teen-agers. We'd miss one another!

Lord, it's a tremendous gift to always be able to
talk to You. There's no time limit on prayer, is
there? No bells that ring, no clocks that sound,
no whistles that blow to tell us that prayer time
is up.

Lord, thanks for sharing thoughts with us through
these pages. And thanks for listening to the
thoughts and ideas from us to You.

Help us always to see that the purpose of prayer
is not to get something but rather to be with
Someone!

Thanks, Lord, for always being with us! Amen.

PRAY, PRAISE, AND HOORAY!

A PRAYER BOOK NEVER ENDS!

NOTICE

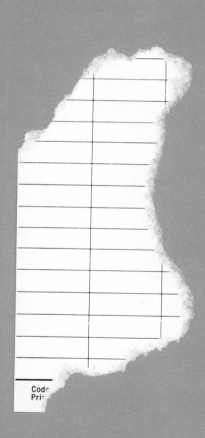

Code
Pri